DUDE, I'M AN A

Dude, I'm An Aspie! Thoughts and Illustrations on Living with Asperger's Syndrome
Matt Friedman

2nd Edition
Copyright 2009, 2012 Matt Friedman

ISBN 978-1-300-02795-9

DUDE, I'M AN ASPIE!

Thoughts and illustrations on living with Asperger's Syndrome

Matt Friedman

Intro

"Dude, I'm An Aspie!" is as a project I put together to disclose my Asperger's to my friends. It was just an attempt to say, "This is who I am," in an informative but fun way. I got such a good response that I decided to share it with a wider audience. The response from fellow Aspies was overwhelmingly positive and touching. They urged me to publish it, so that's what I've done.

I started cartooning at a young age, doodling obsessively on notebook paper in class. It was my special interest, one of the great things about being an Aspie. Piles and piles of creativity, observations, and weirdness, all categorized and meticulously numbered. Today I use cartoons to talk about autism, because it's easier than describing it in words. It's been amazing to reach so many people through my work and hear from fans who feel a connection to it.

A positive outlook and self-image is important for any person on the autism spectrum or who suspects they may be. I believe all deserve to be treated with dignity and compassion. I also believe anyone can, and should, do what I have. That is, to tell your story, your way. My talent is doodling, maybe yours is songwriting, or painting, or whatever. (If it's washing machines, I don't know what to tell you.) But whatever you can do to educate others about Asperger's with your own voice, you will help break down barriers and promote understanding. We can all be advocates.

Now on to the cartoons!

Matt Friedman

My name is Matt and I have Asperger's syndrome. What's that mean, you ask? Well, you're in luck, cause I've made this helpful guide!

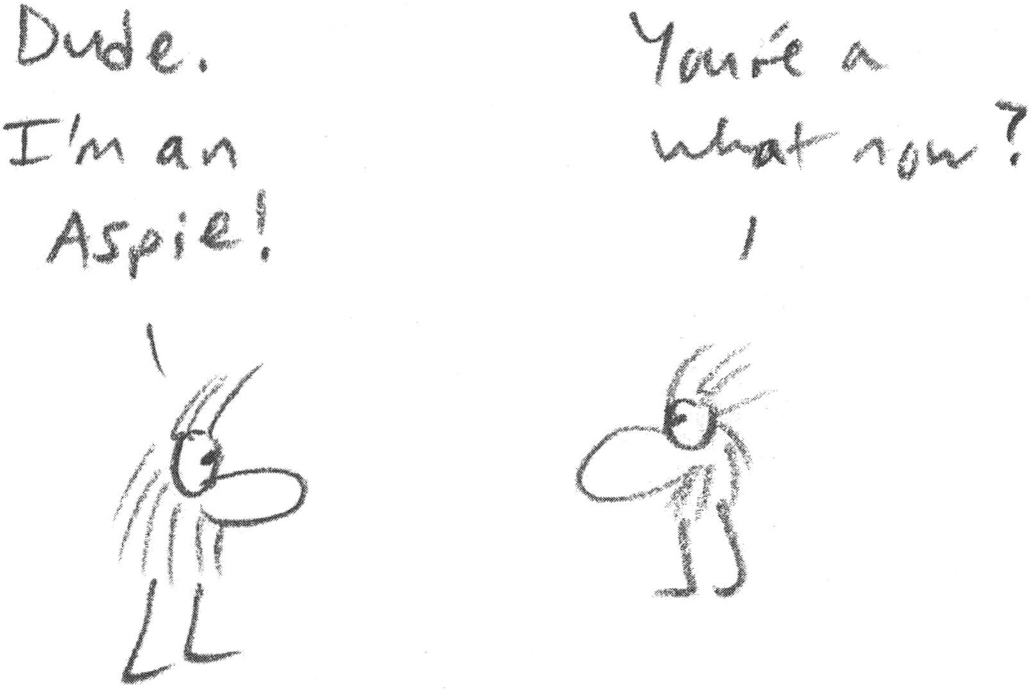
Dude. I'm an Aspie!
You're a what now?

Asperger's is part of the autism spectrum. It has many characteristics, but generally we have difficulty knowing what someone is thinking, explaining our thoughts verbally, and interacting socially with our peers. It is sometimes described as having "a dash of autism."

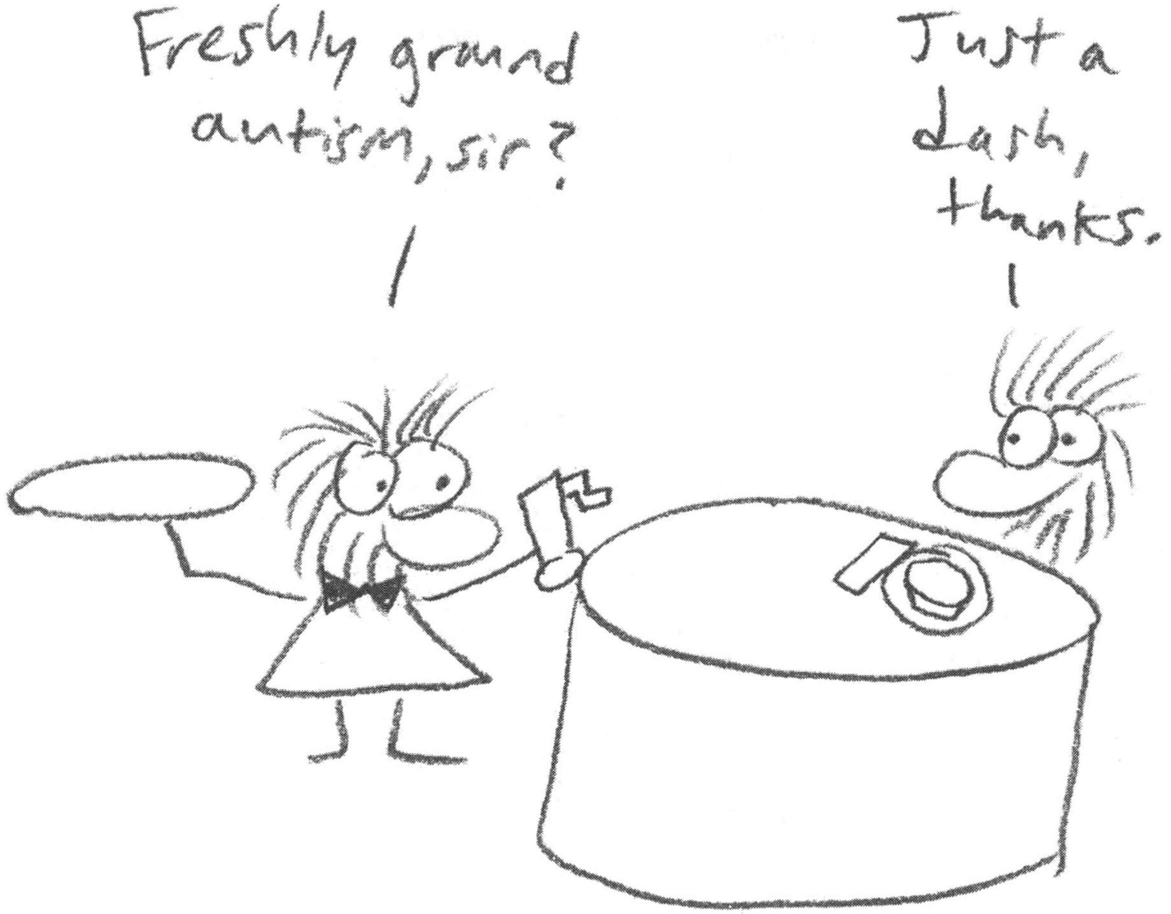
Freshly ground autism, sir?
Just a dash, thanks.

Asperger's is not a disease, it is a genetic variation and a neurological condition. Though I've just recently discovered I have it, I always have and always will. Some say it is a gift, and even vital to human evolution.

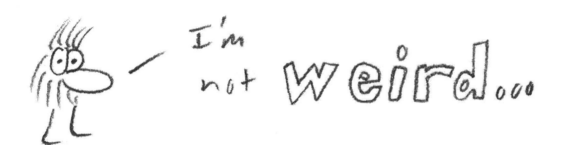

I'm not **weird**...

I'm just **wired** differently!

Asperger's is sometimes called Wrong Planet syndrome. This is because we feel like we come from a different culture and have a different way of perceiving the world. [1]

[1] Attwood 2007, p. 77

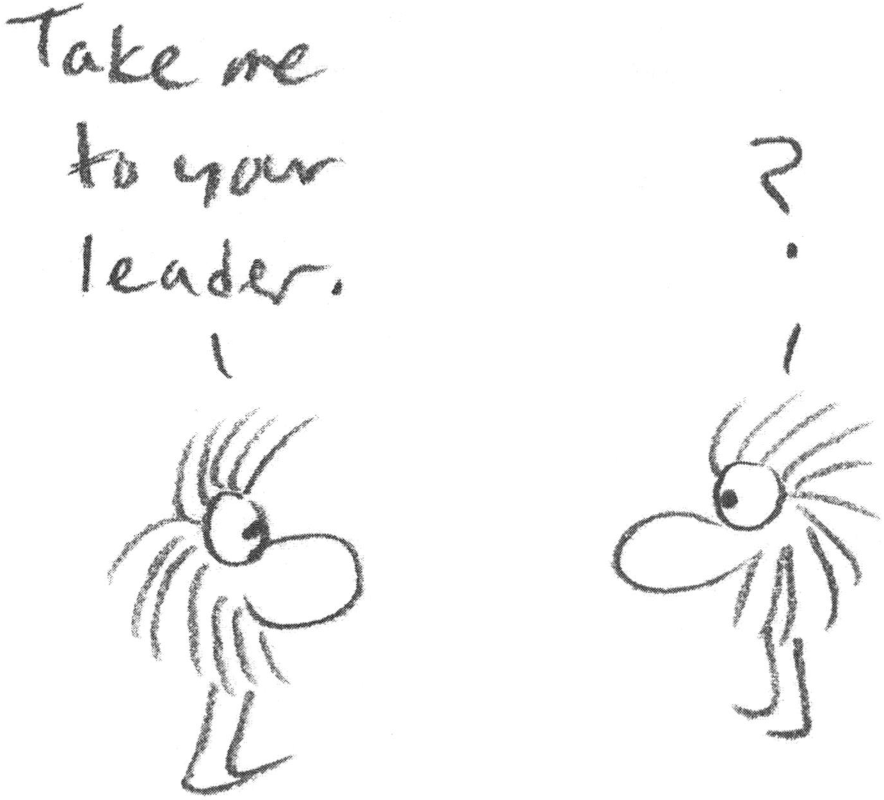
Take me to your leader.
?

Once I learned what Asperger's is, I knew it described me. It answered a lot of questions and explained why I am the way I am. So it was kind of good news! Like finding a box I fit in.

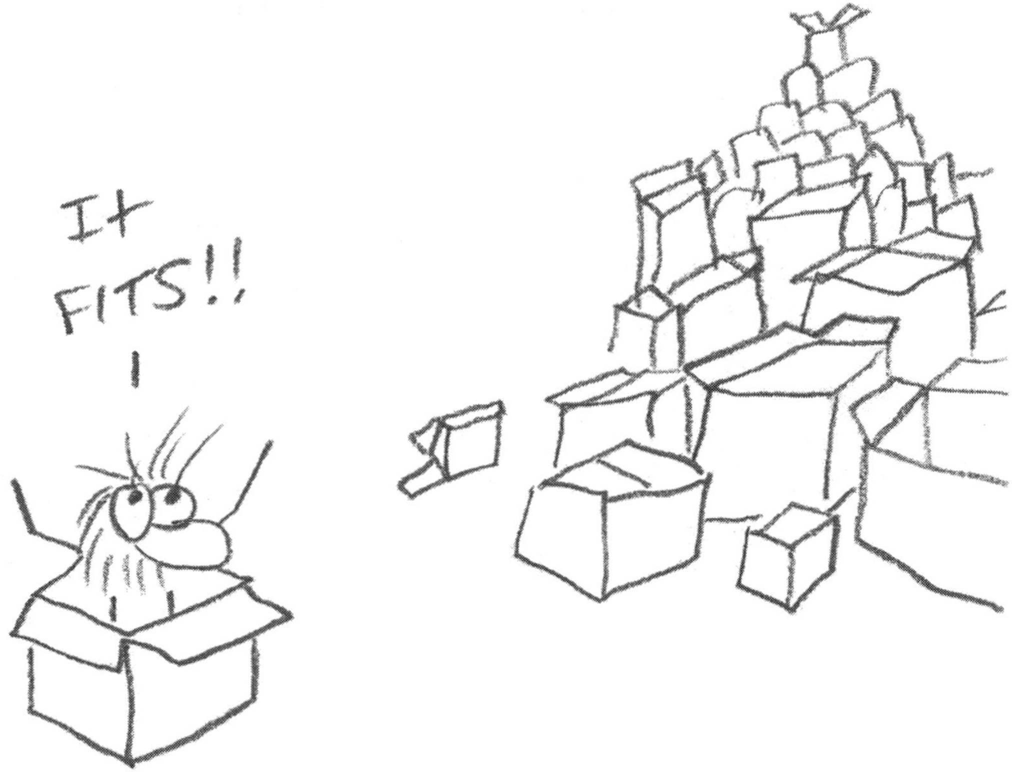
It
FITS!!

Now for some myths and facts: First, I will not look you in the eye for long periods or when I'm talking to you. This is not to be rude. It's because it is the only way I can concentrate on what you're saying.

Lookit me when I'm talkin' to you!
Oh yeh? Well, don't interrupt me when I'm listenin' to you!

In social situations, I don't process information as fast as you. Facial expressions, gestures, and tone of voice all convey subtle information to our brain. The more people who are present, the more info there is to process.

Company.

A crowd.

Crowd-ed.

Get
me out
of here!

Likewise, I don't like crowds and noisy places. This is too much information to take in and causes sensory overload.

Shoppers, 10% off on strawwwwwberries!
Waaaahh!
Ring Ring!
...takin' care o' BIZ-ness...
And then I says to her...

Sometimes we have super-senses. This makes us easily distractible to background noise, a sudden loud noise, or unpleasant odors.

Now, I have something very important to tell you, so listen carefully...
He smells like pepperoni.

If I run into you somewhere I don't expect to, I probably won't recognize you right away. This is called faceblindness. Even though I know what you look like, my mental picture of you is strongly tied to context, your voice, and how other people interact with you.

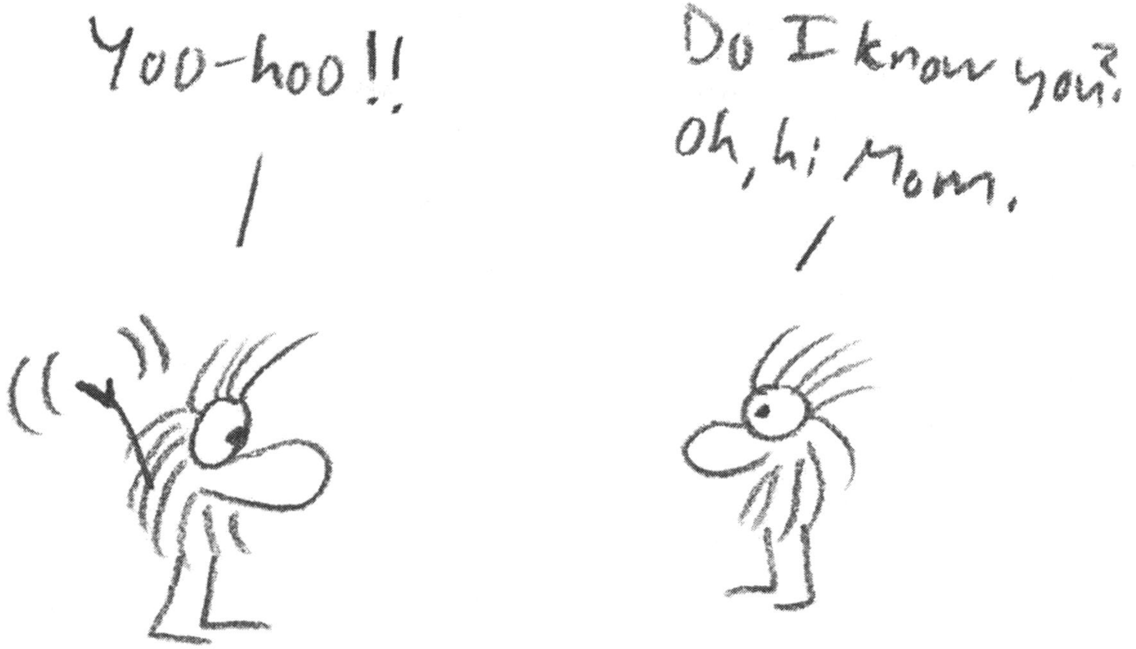
Yoo-hoo!!
Do I know you?
Oh, hi Mom.

Sometimes I interpret things literally, or I can't tell when you're being sarcastic. This is a neurological delay in reading your tone of voice.

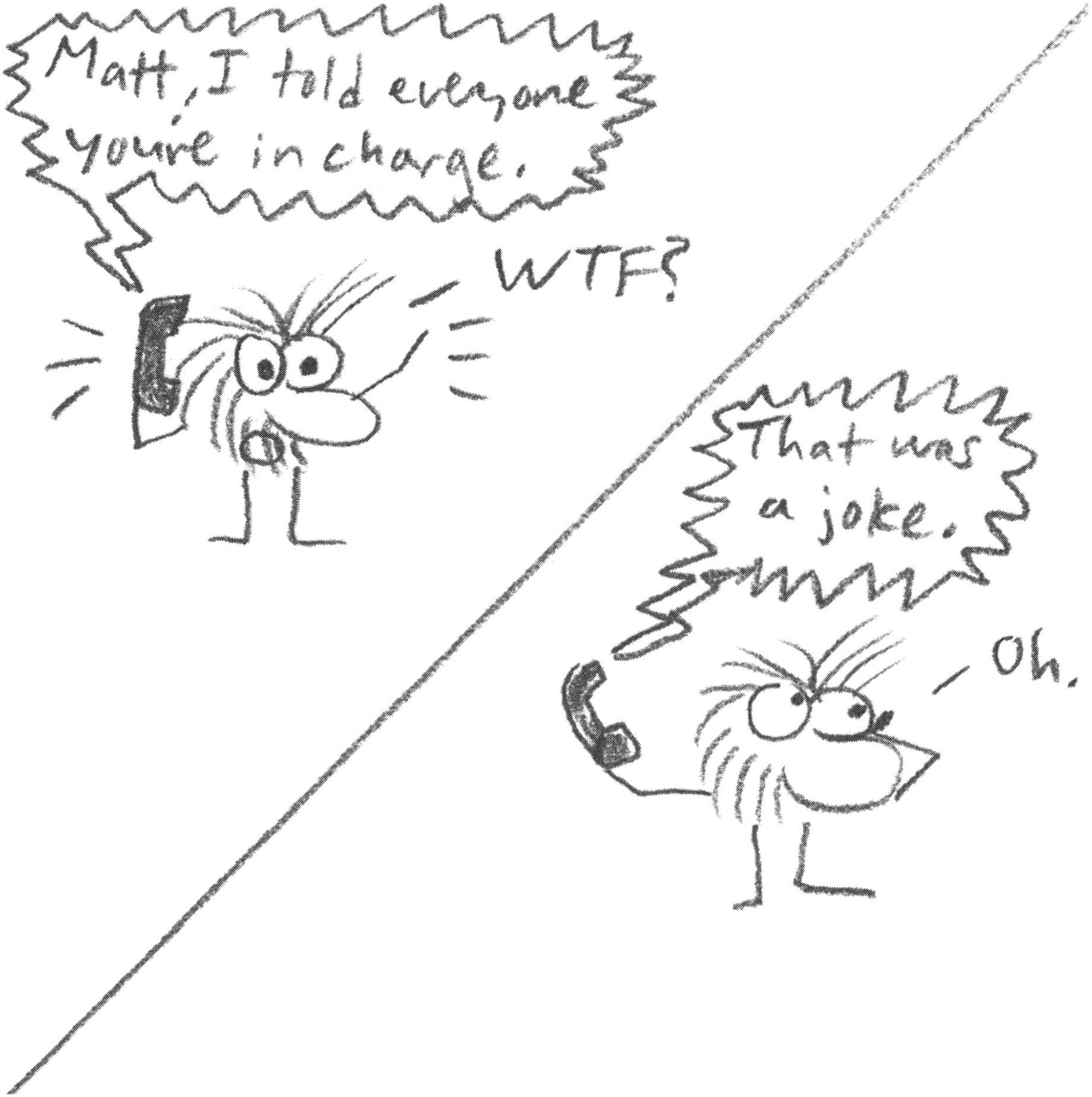
Matt, I told everyone you're in charge.
WTF?
That was a joke.
Oh.

For neurotypical people (that's you), socializing with others relieves your stress or makes you feel energized. We Aspies are the opposite way. Conversation can wear us out, and we often need alone time to "recharge our batteries."

LIFE
100%
100%
10%
That was an awesome meeting!
Yeh, we got so much done!
I need a 1UP!

We usually have special topics or hobbies that we like to pursue with intense concentration and on our own. Examples include trains, foreign cultures, and washing machines.

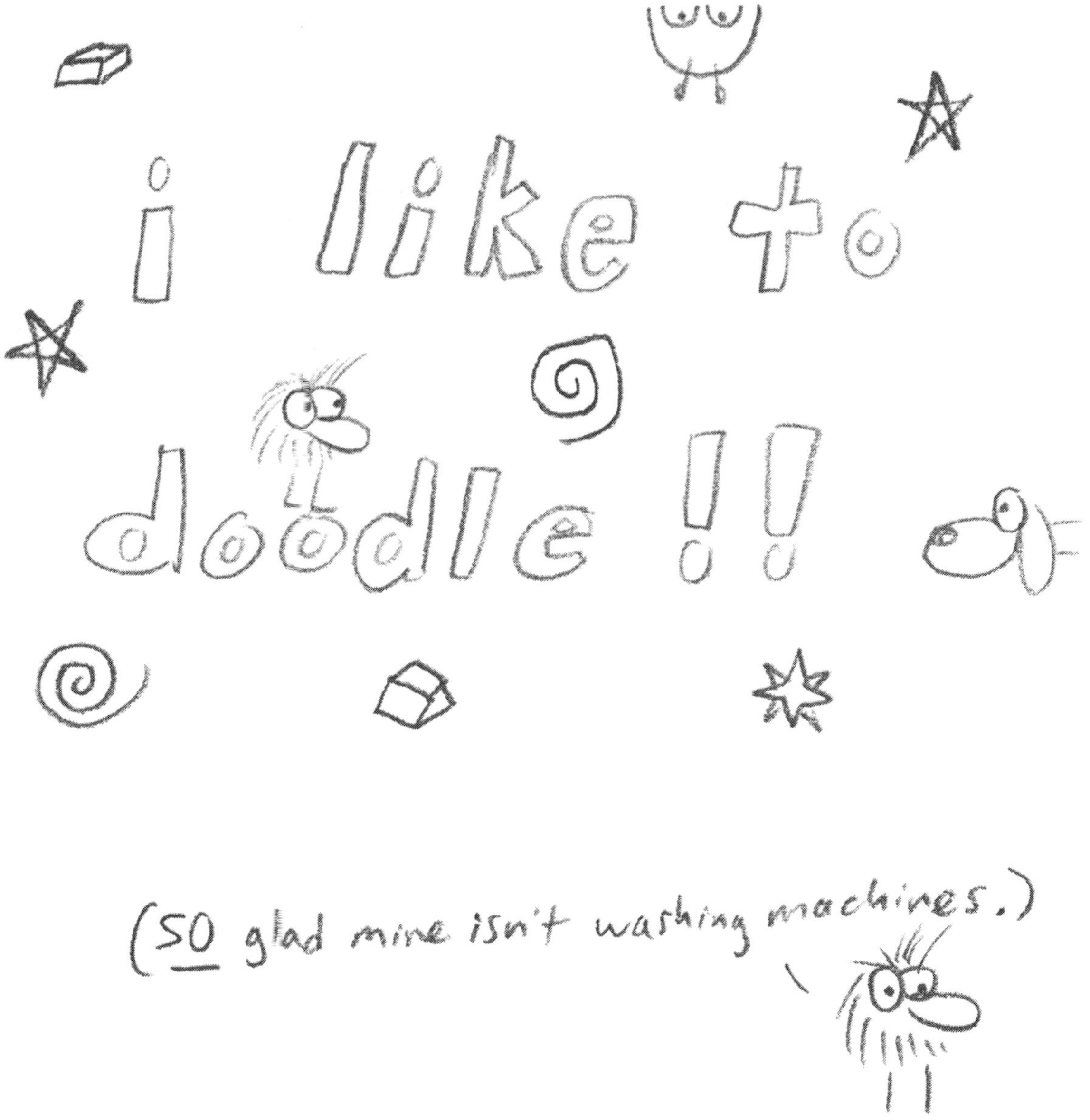
i like to
doodle!!
(SO glad mine isn't washing machines.)

Are there advantages to being an Aspie? Yes! We are honest, detail-oriented, good listeners, and have a unique view of things. Often, we achieve high levels of success in our special interest area.

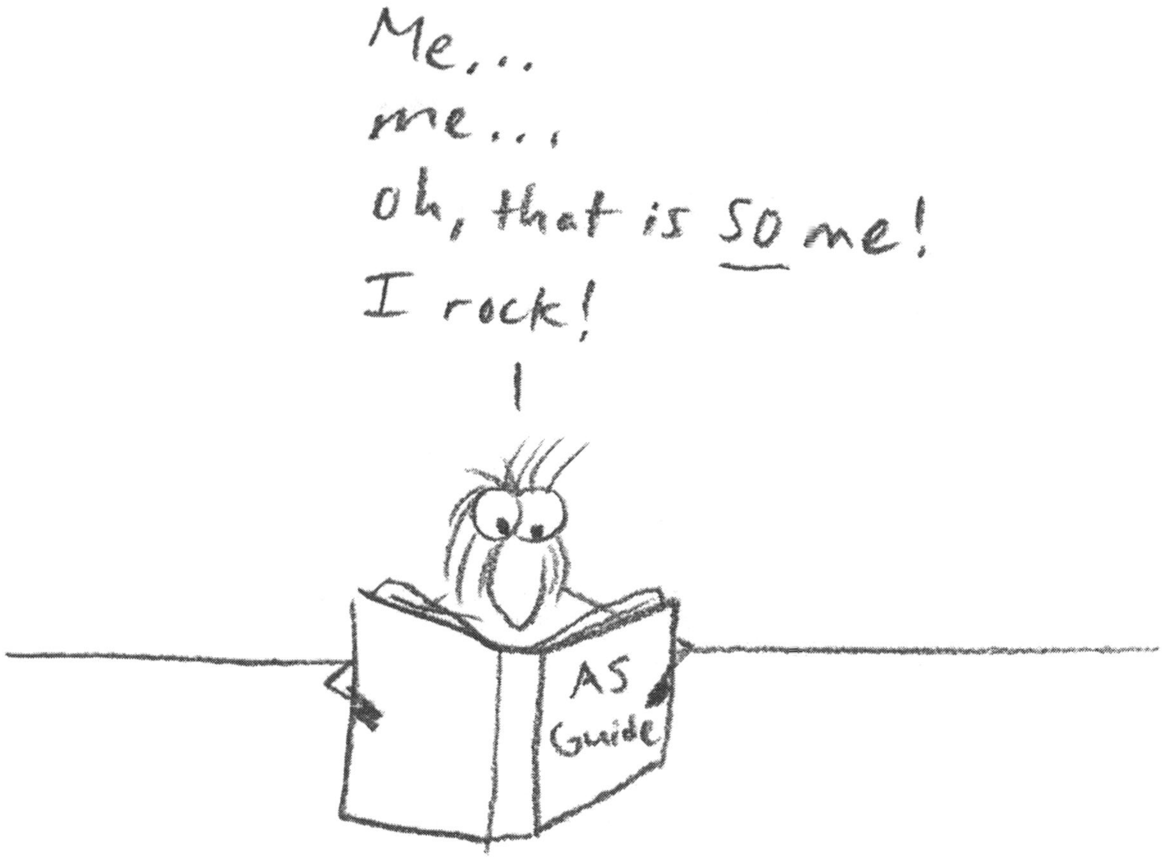
Me...
me...
oh, that is SO me!
I rock!
AS Guide

So that is a glimpse into my world. I hope it has helped you better understand me and others like me. We are all different, and with all differences, knowledge brings understanding. If we understand each other, then there won't be any need for a right planet or a wrong planet. ☺

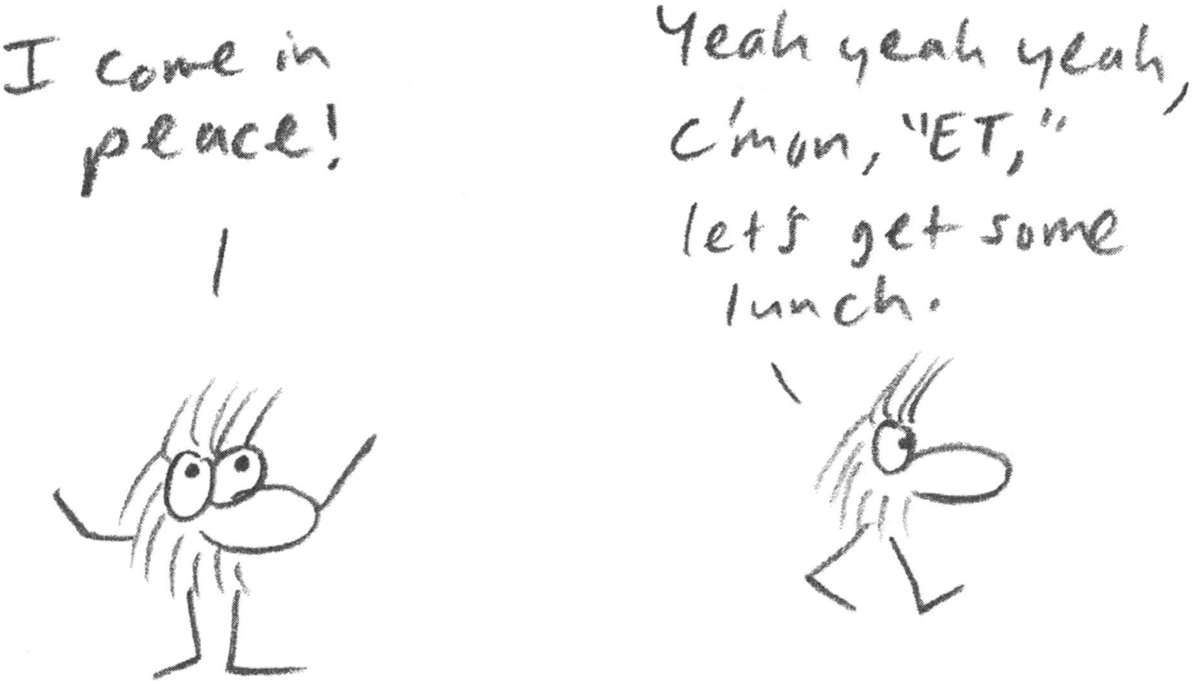
I come in peace!
Yeah yeah yeah, c'mon, "ET," let's get some lunch.

Further Information

Books

Attwood, Tony. <u>The Complete Guide to Asperger's Syndrome</u>. London: Jessica Kingsley Publishers, 2007.

Carley, Michael John. <u>Asperger's from the Inside Out.</u> New York: Penguin Group, 2008.

Grandin, Temple. <u>Thinking In Pictures: My Life with Autism.</u> New York: Vintage Books, 1995.

Web Sites

Autism Blogs Directory. <u>autismblogsdirectory.blogspot.com</u>

thAutcast: A Blogazine for the Aspergers and Autism Community. <u>thautcaust.com/drupal5</u>

The Thinking Person's Guide to Autism. <u>thinkingautismguide.com</u>

Wrong Planet: The online resource & community for Autism & Asperger's. <u>wrongplanet.net</u>

For more thoughts and illustrations, please visit <u>dudeimanaspie.com</u>.

About the Author

Matt Friedman is an autism advocate, cartoonist, writer, and nonprofit fundraiser/marketer. Since 2009, he has authored the blog "Dude, I'm An Aspie," depicting life with Asperger's syndrome with honesty and humor. Matt self-identified as an Aspie in his mid-thirties. Recognizing his obsessive doodling in elementary school had been a special interest, he returned to drawing after 20 years. The first "Dude" cartoon was his own disclosure of Asperger's to friends and family.

Professionally, Matt has worked as a grant writer, fundraiser, and marketer for over 10 years. He received his B.S. in Chemical Engineering from Johns Hopkins University in 1997, but his interest in writing and service led him to the non-profit field. He is a believer in storytelling as a means of opening minds and advocating for a cause. Matt resides in Newark, Delaware, where in his spare time, he enjoys volunteering at a nearby independent living/farming community of adults with autism, messaging with friends, and obsessing over his favorite cartoon shows.

Printed in Great Britain
by Amazon.co.uk, Ltd.,
Marston Gate.